World Issues

REFUGEES

Clive Gifford

Thameside Press

WORLD ISSUES

DRUGS
EQUAL OPPORTUNITIES
GENETIC ENGINEERING
POVERTY
REFUGEES

Produced by Roger Coote Publishing
Gissing's Farm, Fressingfield, Suffolk IP21 5SH, UK

Distributed in the United States by
Smart Apple Media
1980 Lookout Drive
North Mankato, MN 56003

Commissioning Editor: Jason Hook
Designer: Sarah Crouch
Consultant: Jim Mulligan, CSV
Picture Researcher: Lynda Lines

ISBN: 1-931983-27-5
Library of Congress Control Number: 2002 141373

Printed in Hong Kong/China
10 9 8 7 6 5 4 3 2 1

Picture Acknowledgements
We wish to thank the following individuals and organizations for their help and assistance, and for
supplying material in their collections: AKG 16; AP 8 (Dusan Vranic), 20 (Donald Stampfli), 22
(Laurent Gillieron), 31 (Ramon de la Rocha), 34 (PA); Corbis 17 (Hulton-Deutsch), 18 (Hulton-
Deutsch); Hulton Getty 12; Panos 7 (Clive Shirley), 14 (Howard J Davies), 23 (Crispin Highes), 37
(Liba Taylor), 47 (Maya Kardum); Popperfoto 30 (Reuters), 33 (Reuters); Rex Features 10 (Michael
Yassukovic), 13 (Albert Facelly), 15, 25 (Duroux), 26 (Alexandra Boulat), 35, 36 (McMillan), 38, 39
(Dennis Stone), 45 (Sipa); Still Pictures front cover (Heine Pedersen), 4 (Nigel Dickinson), 24 (Heine
Pedersen), 28 (Jorgen Schytte), 32 (Peter Frischmoth), 42 (David Hoffman), 43 (Mike Schroder);
UNHCR front cover main image (L Boscardi), 1 (M Vanappelghem), 3 (H Timmermans), 5 top (H J
Davies), 5 middle (M Vanappelghem), 5 bottom, 6, 11 (L Boscardi), 19 (T Bølstad), 21 (H J Davies),
27, 29, 40 (R Lemoyne), 41, 44 (B Press), 46 (H J Davies). Artwork by Michael Posen. The pictures
used in this book do not show the actual people named in the case studies in the text.

CONTENTS

Knowbuddy Resources 3/03

Mina's Story

Mina is a European refugee now living in the U.S. As a teenager, she was forced to flee her home in Bosnia, part of the former Yugoslavia, during fighting among different ethnic groups.

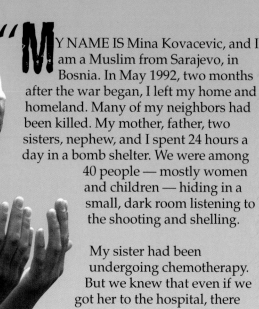

"MY NAME IS Mina Kovacevic, and I am a Muslim from Sarajevo, in Bosnia. In May 1992, two months after the war began, I left my home and homeland. Many of my neighbors had been killed. My mother, father, two sisters, nephew, and I spent 24 hours a day in a bomb shelter. We were among 40 people — mostly women and children — hiding in a small, dark room listening to the shooting and shelling.

My sister had been undergoing chemotherapy. But we knew that even if we got her to the hospital, there would be no treatment for her. So we decided to try to leave. Our car and others were stopped by Serb soldiers. They ordered us to pull off to the side of the road and told us we were being held as hostages. The soldiers began making lists of the children in our convoy, threatening to kill them first.

We spent three nights in our car without food. We saw and heard men being tortured by the soldiers. At night, the soldiers would shine flashlights into our cars while bragging of all the children they had already killed. We were all in terror for my four-year-old nephew.

Finally, we were allowed to go. When we reached Croatia, the Croats put us into a refugee camp where we lived with 40 people to a tent. The Croats were not prepared to receive so many people, and after 10 days they told us we had to move on to another camp in eastern Slovenia.

We were the first refugees to arrive in this camp. There were a few huts, and we were lucky enough to be put into one, although we shared it with 12 or 14 strangers. We felt much safer because there was no shooting in the area. But as summer turned into the fall, more refugees arrived. The huts were full, so new arrivals were housed in tents facing rain, snow, and extreme cold without any heat. Sanitation was deplorable: 20 to 30 toilets and only 20 showers for 3,000 people."

After these experiences, Mina was lucky. Her family was granted refuge in Denmark, and Mina received a scholarship to study in the U.S. She described this as "the greatest thing I could imagine." She has completed a degree in Psychology and hopes to return to her homeland if the situation there remains stable.

Refugees on three continents

Mina is just one of many millions of refugees found all over the world. Many face an uncertain future.

ASIA
The forced labor and forced relocation of ethnic minorities in Myanmar (Burma) has created more than 380,000 refugees and asylum seekers, mainly in Thailand (left), Bangladesh, and India. Refugees are escaping from rape, torture, and murder.

LATIN AMERICA
Civil war and abuses of human rights in Guatemala generated over 120,000 refugees in the 1980s. The majority of these refugees fled to Mexico (left), and some are still housed in refugee camps today.

AFRICA
In 2001, a third of the world's refugees were Africans. There are over 400,000 refugees from Sierra Leone alone. Some camps for these refugees in Guinea (left) and Liberia have been attacked and numbers of refugees have been killed.

What Is A Refugee?

First and foremost, a refugee is a person — and one in need of help. Refugees are people who have fled their home country due to fear. This can be fear of a war close by —or fear of attack from government and military troops due to the religion refugees practice, the politics they believe in, or simply the racial group to which they belong.

This mother and child are refugees from Burundi, in Africa, who have made their way to a refugee camp in the neighboring country of Rwanda.

Asylum seekers are often housed in detention centers, such as this one at Eisenhuttenstadt in Germany.

Defining a refugee

A refugee is a person who, "owing to a well-founded fear of being persecuted for reasons of race, religion, nationality, membership in a particular social group, or political opinion, is outside the country of his [or her] nationality, and is unable to — or, owing to such fear, is unwilling to — avail himself [or herself] of the protection of that country."

Source: The 1951 Convention on the Status of Refugees

THE MOST IMPORTANT definition of a refugee is that given in the 1951 Convention on the Status of Refugees *(see panel)*. Why? Because it is the definition used by many countries and international organizations to determine whether someone is a refugee or not. To be a refugee, you have to be outside your country of origin. Your fear of persecution also has to be "well-founded," which means that you have already experienced persecution or are likely to if you return.

What is a migrant?

People move around from country to country and have done so for thousands of years. This movement is called migration, and the people who move are known as migrants. When people leave their own country to settle in another, they are called emigrants. When they arrive in a new country, they are referred to as immigrants. Many people choose to move countries in the hope of finding work, better prospects, or a higher standard of living. These people are not refugees according to international law. Instead, they are known as economic migrants. They choose to leave their home, often at a time that suits them, and often with their family and possessions. Unlike migrants, refugees cannot return home safely if they wish, and cannot rely on the protection of the authorities in their own country.

What is an asylum seeker?

Asylum seekers are people who have applied for refugee status and are waiting to see if they will get protection as a refugee. Refugees usually ask for, and are granted, protection from a host country before they arrive in it. Asylum seekers tend to ask for protection only after arriving in the host country. In many countries, asylum seekers can be held by the immigration authorities and are not entitled to certain benefits.

Taliban fighters drive through the front line during the war in Afghanistan, as they defect and join the Northern Alliance force opposing the Taliban. As soldiers, they cannot be called refugees.

Can soldiers be refugees?

Only civilians can be refugees. Someone who was once a soldier can qualify, but a person who continues to take part in military activity cannot be considered a refugee. Neither can those who took part in war crimes, such as large-scale human rights abuses during a war. Sometimes, in large refugee camps, authorities suspect that a small number of soldiers and war criminals are present, but find it difficult to identify and remove them.

A criminal who has received a fair trial for an illegal offense, such as theft or assault, is unlikely to be considered a refugee if he or she flees from a country to escape being put into jail. However, some people are imprisoned on false charges and persecuted due to their race, politics, or religion. They may well have a case for being refugees.

Can you be a refugee at home?

Many people are forced to flee their homes, but do not travel across the border that separates their country from another. This means that they may be homeless, seeking safety and in grave danger — potentially from their own government — but they are still within their own country. The term for someone in this situation is "internally displaced person" or IDP. Sudan, in northeast Africa, has been ravaged by civil war for over 20 years, and has four million IDPs. Colombia, in South

America, has over two million. IDPs are the fastest-growing type of people displaced from their homes, yet they are also those with the fewest rights. Many international agreements on refugees apply only to people who have crossed their own country's borders, although aid organizations do sometimes have the chance to assist IDPs.

How many refugees are there?

Refugees are not a few small groups of unfortunate people as they amount to millions of the world's population. In 1951, there were an estimated over two million refugees in the world, and just over half this number were found in Europe. By 1981, the total figure had rocketed to 10.1 million, and by 1991 to 17 million refugees. These are just some of the millions of people uprooted from

their homes and forced into a precarious way of life. Refugees, asylum seekers, IDPs — all these different types of people are considered to be "at risk" by the UN. Of the 21.8 million people considered at risk at the start of 2001, almost 10 million were children.

The world picture in the year 2000

Percentage of refugees hosted by region:
Asia: 44.6 percent
Africa: 30 percent
Europe: 19.3 percent
North America: 5.2 percent
Oceania: 0.6 percent
Latin America/Caribbean: 0.3 percent

This map shows the country of origin of the ten largest refugee populations in 1999, in order of size.

KEY
1 Afghanistan
2 Burundi
3 Iraq
4 Sudan
5 Bosnia–Herzegovina
6 Somalia
7 Angola
8 Sierra Leone
9 Eritrea
10 Vietnam
Note: this list does not include an estimated nearly four million Palestinians.

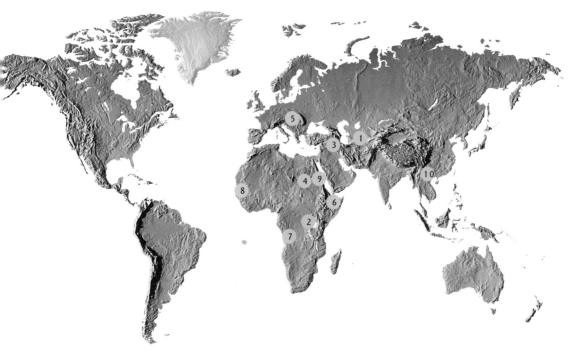

What Causes Refugees?

According to the UN, one in every 115 people in the world has been forced to flee. Each individual has his or her own reasons for becoming a refugee, but there are some typical causes. These include abuse of human rights and persecution because of political opinions, race, or religious beliefs. But one of the most common of all causes is war.

WAR, WITH ITS horrors and dangers, causes many of the millions of asylum seekers and IDPs found throughout the world. International bodies such as the UN believe that persons fleeing war and war-related conditions should be considered refugees, especially if their own country cannot or will not protect them.

Some wars are fought between different countries. Others are civil wars, fought largely within the borders of one nation, between those in power, and those seeking power. Since the Second World War, civil wars have been fought on almost every continent. They are often extremely bloody conflicts, which last a long time and can tear countries apart.

A Chechen fighter during the 1994 war in Grozny. The conflict created terrible destruction and loss of human life, and created thousands of asylum seekers.

Afghan children at New Shamshatoo refugee camp, in Pakistan, line up in front of their makeshift school. The tents and basic education were provided by the UNHCR, a part of the United Nations.

Civil wars can start when a regional group fights, not for total control of a country, but for independence from the rest of the country. The 1991 break-up of the Soviet Union saw a number of independent countries created. When the people of Chechnya also wanted independence, they declared Chechnya a separate state. The Russian Federation, of which Chechnya was a part, responded in 1994 by invading. War devastated the capital city, Grozny, and thousands fled the fighting.

Why does war create refugees?

For those people in, or near, a war zone, the fear and suffering can be intense. Shelling may destroy buildings; loved ones can die, disappear, or be seriously injured; and the most basic human needs, such as the provision of food and fresh water, may no longer be available. Armed forces moving through an area frequently take what they want from people in towns and villages. They sometimes rape, kill and beat innocent civilians.

All over the world, the very real and terrifying threat of war being visited on a person's homeland is often enough to force them to take flight. Following the destruction of the twin towers of New York's World Trade Center by terrorists on September 11, 2001 retaliation was launched by the armed forces of the U.S. and its allies against Afghanistan. This military action prompted over a million people to flee their homes.

Asians from Uganda arrive at Stansted Airport, near London, in 1972. Thousands of Ugandan Asians were forced to flee from the brutal regime of the dictator Idi Amin.

How do governments create refugees?

There have been occasions when a government has deliberately used policies of murder and persecution to force a minority out of a country. One of the most infamous examples occurred in the African nation of Uganda. When Major-General Idi Amin took control of Uganda in 1971, he declared that all Asians should leave, and their property should be seized. Most had settled there from India generations earlier, and many were wealthy and well-educated. Over 30,000 fled the country, a large number of them to Britain. A number of those who stayed behind were murdered.

What is genocide?

Genocide means committing acts with intent to destroy, in whole or in part, a national, ethnic, racial, or religious group. The term was invented to describe the extermination of Jewish peoples by Nazi Germany during the Second World War. Genocide is deliberate, planned, brutal, and terrifying. It can involve assault, murder, and the use of force to remove children from a group.

One of the most horrific examples of genocide in recent times occurred in the African nation of Rwanda. In 1994, almost a million men, women, and children of the minority Tutsi peoples were slaughtered by the ruling Hutus. The need to escape from this genocide led to the creation of hundreds of thousands of refugees.

Is it an endless cycle?

Some wars do come to a peaceful conclusion, with both sides agreeing to attempt to resolve their differences. But more and more conflicts do not have a neat end. Conflict and violence quieten down for a time, then flare up again. Renewed war in Chechnya in 1999, for example, generated 600,000 refugees, this cycle of violence creating refugees on both sides. After the genocide in Rwanda, a civil war saw the Tutsis wrestle power from the majority Hutus. A million Rwandans, mainly Hutus, immediately crossed into Zaire because they feared retaliation.

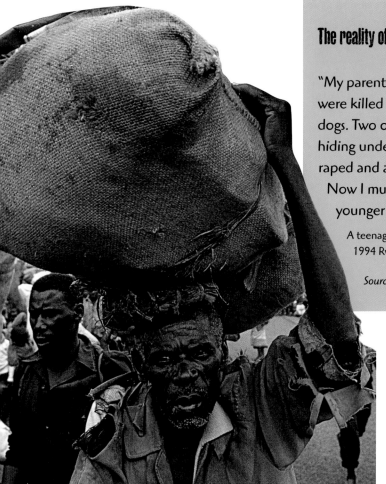

The reality of genocide

"My parents, five brothers and sisters were killed and their bodies eaten by dogs. Two of my sisters survived by hiding underneath the bodies. I was raped and a baby boy was born. Now I must look after him, two younger sisters, and a brother."

A teenage survivor of the 1994 Rwandan genocide.

Source: Refugees magazine (UNHCR)

A refugee from the Hutu peoples of Rwanda carries all his remaining possessions as he travels towards safety.

What are human rights?

Human rights are a collection of basic freedoms and protections which international organizations believe every person should have. The word "should" is important, because many people are actually deprived of these rights. The abuse of human rights is a major reason for people seeking refuge in another country.

In 1948, the UN produced the document called the Universal Declaration of Human Rights. It describes a number of basic rights essential for humans to live properly. Some of these are known as social and economic rights, such as the right to work. Others are even more fundamental. Articles 3 to 18 cover civil rights — freedoms that belong to every individual. These include the right to life, the right to a fair trial, and the right to seek asylum. Article 18 states that everyone has the right to freedom of thought, conscience, and religion.

In many countries, people are deprived of their civil rights. They may be arrested at will, imprisoned without a fair trial, or forced into slavery. They may be imprisoned and beaten just because they hold political or religious beliefs which are different to those of the authorities.

Why are people tortured?

Article 5 of the Universal Declaration of Human Rights states that: "No one shall be subjected to torture or to cruel, inhuman or degrading treatment or punishment." Yet, every year thousands of people are subjected to torture, often by the authorities of the country that is supposed to protect them.

Palden Gyatso, a monk from Tibet, campaigns against torture by the gates of COPEX, one of the world's most important arms fairs. Gyatso spent 33 years in Chinese prisons and labor camps for campaigning for Tibetan independence from China.

Some American prisons are attracting attention from human rights organizations for their tough regimes. Teenage prisoners may be given few or no personal possessions, almost no exercise time, and long periods of solitary confinement.

Torture is used to punish, to intimidate, or to obtain confessions to crimes. It can involve beatings, electric shocks, and depriving people of sleep, food, or use of a toilet. Some victims die, and those who survive are left with emotional and physical scars for the rest of their lives.

Where do human rights abuses occur?

Human rights abuses do not just occur in poor, developing countries. The files of human rights groups such as Amnesty International include many cases from wealthy, developed nations — including the U.S., Germany, and Britain. Some teenagers in high-security prisons in the U.S. are allowed just four

Victim of torture

The Tamils are a minority people in Sri Lanka. Ravi Sundaralingam, a Tamil, was a victim of torture for many months. Soldiers blindfolded him, hung him upside down by his ankles and beat him with iron bars. Once, they lit a fire underneath his head. At other times, they applied electric shocks to his genitals.

Source: New Internationalist

hours a week outside of their cells. In Australia, 115 Aborigines died in police or prison custody between 1990 and 1999. In France, some soldiers admitted to having used severe torture.

Have There Always Been Refugees?

Refugees are not just a twenty-first century problem. The same causes which create modern refugees, such as religious persecution and war, have generated refugees for thousands of years.

THE TERM REFUGEE was first used over 300 years ago to describe a group of people in France known as the Huguenots. The French king, Louis XIV, was a Roman Catholic who was opposed to the Protestant beliefs of the Huguenots. Persecution of the group started in the 1680s. They were forbidden to worship in the way they chose and to leave France. But the Huguenots escaped in huge numbers, and almost a fifth of France's population left the country. Many arrived in England, where the word "refugee" was applied to them. It came from the French verb *réfugier*, which means to take or seek refuge.

Huguenot refugees left France and traveled to many different European countries. Here, refugees are received by Prince Friedrich Wilhelm of Brandenburg (which is now part of Germany).

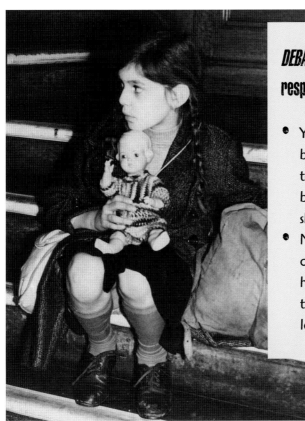

DEBATE - Should countries be held responsible for their past?

DEBATE - Should countries be held responsible for their past?

- Yes. Some of the problems created by the colonial powers still exist today. These countries became rich by exploiting their colonies. They should pay back this "historic debt."
- No. People in countries that were once colonial powers should not be held responsible for the actions of their ancestors. It happened too long ago to be relevant today.

This Jewish girl is just one of 5,000 refugees who arrived in Britain from Nazi Germany in 1938.

Long before this, there were refugees. The founding figures of two major religions were refugees. In the Christian faith it is believed that the Son of God, Jesus Christ, was taken during his infancy to Egypt to escape the persecution of King Herod, the ruler of Palestine. Six centuries later, Mohammed, the founder of Islam, fled the oppression of the Meccans. He left Makkah (Mecca) and journeyed to a place which was later called Al Madinah (Medina). This flight to safety, known as the Hegira, is commemorated by Muslims to this day.

Who were the colonial powers?

From the sixteenth century onward, European countries explored other lands and claimed them as their colonies. The colonial powers — such as the French, Dutch, British, Spanish, and Portuguese — divided up continents between them. In doing so, especially in Africa, they ignored tribal and ethnic boundaries that had existed before their arrival. Many examples of exploitation and oppression occurred under colonial rule, and territorial borders marked out for the convenience of the European countries have continued to create conflict and refugees to this day.

Did anything change in modern times?

Religious and ethnic persecution has always been one of the main causes of refugees. This remained true in the twentieth century. In their persecution and attempted extermination of the Jewish population of Europe, the Nazis created hundreds of thousands of refugees. These included 10,000 children who were separated from their families in 1938–39, and sent out of German-occupied lands.

How has the refugee problem changed?

In the past, movement from one country to another did not require passports and visas — and the right to asylum was commonly recognized and honoured. It was only as more frontiers and boundaries became fixed and closed, in the late nineteenth and the twentieth centuries, that refugees with nowhere to go became a serious problem.

Another twentieth-century development was the great increase in the number of refugees created due to people being persecuted, tortured, and threatened with death because of their political opinions. Around one-and-a-half million opponents of communism left Russia between the start of the Russian Revolution in 1917 and the end of the civil war in 1921. During the 1936–39 Spanish Civil War, more than 200,000 Spaniards loyal to the king fled from Spain. The aftermath of the Second World War saw the greatest ever movement of people in Europe. Somewhere between 30 and 50 million people — many of them prisoners of war and slave labourers, but mostly refugees — moved between 1945 and 1948.

Have there been famous refugees?

Refugees have made important contributions to the arts and sciences like film actress Marlene Dietrich and Chilean novelist Isabel Allende. The world-famous physicist Albert Einstein became a refugee in 1933 when he left

Leading a mule loaded with children and possessions, this Spanish family were among thousands forced to leave their home during the Spanish Civil War.

The Dalai Lama

In 1959, the spiritual and political leader of Tibet, the Dalai Lama Tenzin Gyatso, was forced to become a refugee. A popular uprising by Tibetans was crushed by the Chinese military which had occupied the country since 1950. Granted asylum in India, the Dalai Lama has worked tirelessly for a peaceful solution, based on tolerance, to the problems in Tibet. For his work in human rights, his rejection of violence, and his ideas for solving international conflicts, he was awarded the 1989 Nobel Peace Prize.

Berlin for the U.S. after Nazi Germany began its harassment of Jews. He was followed by other notable Jews, including the composer Bela Bartok and the novelist Thomas Mann.

The powerful position of American Secretary of State has been held twice by a refugee. Henry Kissinger, who held the post from 1973 to 1977, was a refugee from the Nazis. Madeleine Albright, who in 1996 became the first female Secretary of State, had escaped twice from her home nation of Czechoslovakia. The first time was in 1939, after Germany had invaded the country. She returned home after the Second World War, but the communist take-over of Czechoslovakia forced Albright's family to leave again, and they were granted asylum in the U.S.

Who Helps Refugees?

If you are an official member of a country or state, you may have many rights and benefits — such as the right to healthcare and education. But what happens when you leave that country? What rights do you have then?

THE INTERNATIONAL COMMUNITY has tried to produce sets of rights for refugees which are agreed in principle worldwide. Turning the theory into action is far more complex and difficult to achieve. Aid agencies, voluntary bodies, charities, and organizations within the UN all seek to assist the millions of refugees and asylum seekers that exist.

Attempts to co-ordinate help for refugees in an international way only started after the First World War. The League of Nations, an international body established in 1920, appointed a Norwegian, Fridtjof Nansen, to be in charge of its efforts to help refugees. Nansen believed in international co-operation. He organized transport,

Jean-Baptiste Richardier, co-founder of Handicap International, a group which assists refugees and campaigns against land mines, receives the Nansen Medal from UNHCR High Commissioner, Sadako Ogata, in 1996. Named after Fridtjof Nansen, the award honours outstanding work with refugees.

Standing in front of the UNHCR symbol, this young child is an internally displaced person (IDP) uprooted from her home in Rwanda.

food supplies, and other forms of assistance to help refugees in Russia, Greece, and elsewhere. He also created a form of travel document known as a Nansen Passport, which gave refugees with no national documents the right to travel safely. In 1922, he won the Nobel Peace Prize for his work.

What is the UNHCR?

The UN was established in 1945, and in 1950 created a department called the Office of the United Nations High Commissioner for Refugees (UNHCR). The following year, representatives from 26 nations met in Geneva, Switzerland. The Second World War had ended six years earlier, yet large numbers of refugees produced by the war still existed, especially in Europe. These refugees had little protection and few rights. Over three weeks, the 26 nations produced the international agreement called the 1951 UN Convention on the Status of Refugees. This defined what a refugee was *(see page 7)* and set out a series of rights for refugees. These included the right not to be returned home against your will and the right to practise your religion and to receive an education in countries of asylum.

Among its many responsibilities, the UNHCR was given the task of policing the Convention on the Status of Refugees, to make sure that it was enforced. It has so far persuaded 140 countries to ratify (sign and agree to) both the original convention, and more recent conventions which extend the series of rights. The UNHCR is working hard to this day to persuade other governments to sign, and to pressure those who have already signed to carry out what the convention states. Many nations have not created the laws or spent the money required to turn rights for refugees into reality.

What has the UNHCR achieved?

In 50 years, the UNHCR has aided and assisted more than 50 million displaced people in need. It has formed partnerships with national governments, charities, and other groups to provide relief aid such as tents, food, and water. It has also offered legal assistance to people trying to gain asylum. The UNHCR sponsors hundreds of programs which help refugees returning home — providing transport, cash grants, farm tools, seeds, and home-building materials. For refugees who cannot return, the UNHCR tries to find new homes either in the asylum country they are in, or in another country where they can resettle.

The UNHCR started life with just 33 staff, and was supposed to be a temporary department. But as new refugee numbers have soared, the UNHCR has grown to over 5,000 staff working in 120 countries. It is funded mainly by voluntary contributions from governments, and in some years does not receive all the money that it should. In 2001, for example, its budget was US$881 million — but this meant it had to cut staff numbers by 16 percent.

What other organizations help refugees?

The United Nations Relief and Works Agency (UNRWA) was set up in 1949 to help Palestinian refugees created by the conflict between Israel and its Arab neighbors. Its work continues today.

Hollywood actress Angeline Jolie, famous for her role in Tomb Raider, was appointed a UNHCR Goodwill Ambassador for refugees in 2001.

DEBATE: Can charities make a difference?

- Yes. Charities raise millions of dollars, and bring relief to many refugees. They also raise awareness of the plight of refugees.
- No. Despite charities, the refugee problem remains. Why has it never been solved? Governments might do more if charities did less.

Therapeutic Feeding Centers, such as this one run by Oxfam in Bulhagarry, Ethiopia, are vital to combat malnutrition and help children and adults regain good health.

A working budget

"The current working budget amounts to less than $40 per year for each person of concern to UNHCR. If any governments feel that UNHCR can effectively operate with less, I would like them to explain how."

UNHCR head, Ruud Lubbers, October 1, 2001.

Source: UNHCR

Looking after the planet's children, 25 million of whom are displaced from their homes, is the role of the United Nations International Children's Emergency Fund (UNICEF).

There are many voluntary organizations and charities which help people suffering from malnutrition, poverty, ill health, or lack of basic rights. Refugees often fall into one or more of these categories.

Large organizations such as the International Red Cross, CARE, and Oxfam provide healthcare, food, water, and shelter directly to emergency areas. Others, such as Amnesty International, campaign for human rights. Voluntary organizations in many countries assist refugees in settling into their new home. They provide advice, counseling, and sometimes financial aid.

What Happens To Refugees?

The decision to become a refugee can involve saying goodbye to all that you know. It is often a sudden decision made amid fear and chaos. What follows is rarely easy or straightforward. Fleeing to safety can involve great hardship, suffering, and even death. To become a refugee, you have to escape your immediate area, reach and cross your country's border, and seek refuge on the other side.

MOST PEOPLE FLEEING their homeland travel on foot and seek shelter along the way. Their journey is often dangerous due to natural hazards. In tropical regions, people in flight risk death from the heat, as well as lack of food or water. In contrast, people fleeing parts of Albania and Chechnya in winter have had to contend with bitter cold and the dangers of pneumonia and hypothermia. People in flight also sometimes have to deal with human hazards. They risk straying into areas of military action, or being attacked and robbed. In certain war-torn countries, large areas are covered with land mines, many of which are unmarked. There are

A long, arduous trek, with little food or water, faces these Ethiopian refugees during a severe drought.

After setting off in boats unsuited to rough waters, these Vietnamese boat people have reached safety. Others were not so lucky: as many as a quarter-of-a-million boat people perished at sea.

Taking flight

"I had to run in just the clothes I stood up in, not knowing where the rest of my family were or what had happened to them. On the way I saw many horrible things, like five small children, burned black. Horrible. I ran through the bush. I stayed for three days without food."

Cecilia, a Sudanese refugee, 1990.

Source: New Internationalist

approximately 110 million land mines lying in wait for the unwary in some 70 countries. The most heavily mined countries include the Sudan, Angola, Cambodia, Croatia, Iraq, and Nicaragua.

While inside their home country and attempting to cross the border, people in flight experience the ever-present fear of being caught and returned home, where they might be imprisoned or executed. During the major refugee crisis in Mozambique, for example, around 2,000 people each month were caught by South African border authorities and forced to return to their home country.

Who were the "boat people?"

Not everyone flees over land or by foot. Some refugees travel in trucks or cars until they reach the border, run out of gas, or have their vehicle taken by police or soldiers. Many refugees also leave by sea, as stowaways or on board their own boats. After communist forces took control of South Vietnam in 1975, thousands of people tried to escape in flimsy fishing boats unsuitable for long sea voyages. Many drowned or were caught by the Vietnamese navy. Yet, by 1978 some 86,000 "boat people," as they became known, had reached Thailand and other countries in Southeast Asia.

Goma, in Zaire, where around 800,000 refugees from Rwanda reached or passed through refugee centers and camps in 1994. At the start of this crisis, there were only 1,500 aid workers to care for them.

What is life like in a refugee camp?

Some refugees sneak over the border and "disappear" into a new country, living on the move or going into hiding. But the majority arrive at relief or transit camps and then move on to refugee camps. Life in a refugee camp can be disorientating, traumatic, and extremely hard. Relief at arriving safely can quickly be replaced by the realization that a refugee camp is far from being the promised land many had imagined.

Despite the best efforts of aid workers and local people, conditions in refugee camps can be appalling. Many refugees arrive ill or injured. With limited medical facilities and often poor sanitation in camps, the risk of disease and infection is high. For example, in July 1994, when one million Rwandan refugees poured into eastern Zaire over four days, more than 50,000 people died of cholera, dysentery, and other diseases. Measles, diarrhea, acute respiratory (breathing) infections, and malaria are also major problems in refugee situations — often causing over 60 percent of deaths. Many of the remaining deaths occur through malnutrition, as camps may not have sufficient supplies to feed everybody.

Organizing a refugee camp is a complex and difficult task. Supplying enough food and fresh water can be a constant problem. In camps for over 200,000 Somali refugees in eastern Ethiopia, for example, often only a quarter of the UNHCR's target of 42 pints of water per refugee each day is obtained.

Finding work for thousands of able-bodied people can be another major concern. Yet, for many refugees, the camp provides safety and hope. Initiatives from charities and organizations, along with the hard work of refugees themselves, help to create schools, work projects, and vital medical facilities.

Where are most refugee camps found?

Over 85 percent of all refugees housed in camps are living outside of Europe and North America. Most refugee camps are in countries neighboring the refugees' country of exile. Frequently, these are poor, developing countries which can barely feed, clothe, and shelter their own people. In 1993, for example, the poor African nation of Malawi was attempting to look after one million refugees from Mozambique — a tenth of its own population.

A teacher uses a tree as a blackboard stand for her class of refugee children. It takes resourcefulness, patience, and hard work to create school and leisure facilities in refugee camps.

This young Palestinian refugee receives his daily meal of sausage and bread given out at the Dhelsheh refugee camp on the West Bank in Israel.

DEBATE: Should permanent refugee camps be set up?

- Yes. The causes of refugees look unlikely to be resolved for a long time, if ever. With international support, permanent camps could be built with proper facilities. People could remain safely in one place, and receive treatment for injury and disease.
- No. Making camps permanent would remove many refugees' greatest hope: returning home. Local peoples in poor countries would also feel resentful when they saw huge amounts of aid pouring into their homeland to create permanent refugee camps.

How long do refugee camps last?

Refugee camps are considered a safety net which should be used as a last resort. They are supposed to be temporary, and in some cases they do close down when refugees return home. But many refugee camps have lasted ten years or more. Camps to house refugees from the troubles in Rwanda were set up in the early 1960s, and some still exist in the twenty-first century.

Palestinian refugee camps have an even longer history. In 1948, Palestine was partitioned (divided up) to create the state of Israel as a homeland for the Jewish people. Not long after its creation, military conflicts started between Israel and a number of neighboring Arab countries which supported the Palestinians. Israel gained territory and hundreds of thousands of Palestinian refugees were created.

In 2000, there were over three million Palestinians in some of the oldest refugee camps in the world.

What is dependency?

The longer a camp holds large numbers of refugees, the greater the problem of dependency becomes. This means that refugees lose control over their own lives and become completely reliant on the assistance of others to live. Young children can grow up through their teenage years and into adulthood knowing no other way of living than being dependent on help from the agencies which run a camp. This can make it exceptionally hard for these people, should they eventually return home or receive permission to resettle in another country.

Refugee camps are often large and sprawling, as this aerial photo of a camp at Kibeho in Rwanda shows.

Memories of a refugee camp

Theogene Rudasingwa was appointed Rwandan ambassador to the U.S. in 1996. Almost the entire first 30 years of his life had been spent in refugee camps:

"My mother, brother and sister had to work long hours in order to get food for the day. After working 12 hours, they gave you a bunch of bananas... When I began learning how to write, it was on our thighs using sharp pieces of wood or grass in order to leave some kind of imprint."

Source: U.S. Committee for Refugees

Tragedy in Budapest

The grisly sight of 18 decomposing bodies found locked inside the refrigerated trailer of a truck was imprinted on the mind of Ditlev Nordgaard. "It was a terrible tragedy," recalled Nordgaard, UNHCR deputy representative in Budapest, Hungary. "You could hardly recognize the faces." The trailer had been locked from the outside, and the 18 were found suffocated. According to police, the ventilation system broke down just after the truck set out from Bulgaria. The refugees had paid US$800 each to a Bulgarian trucker to transport them to Germany and Italy. Most had sold all their possessions in Sri Lanka just to pay for the trip.

Source: Fernando del Mundo/Refugees Magazine

What happens after refugee camps?

Millions of people remain in refugee camps for far longer than they or the authorities had hoped. They are caught in limbo between returning home and forging a new life in another country. But a number of refugees do leave refugee camps either to return home, receive asylum in another country, or make a desperate attempt to find a solution themselves.

Life in a refugee camp can be frustrating and difficult. Because camps are often built on borders, they are vulnerable to attack. Some refugees choose to leave refugee camps and try to survive alone. In isolated parts of Africa and Asia in particular, many refugees roam the land eking out a precarious existence. They work where they can, and often resort to theft and other crimes in order to survive. Some refugees leave camps in order to enter into other countries as illegal immigrants. For example, the Sangatte refugee camp near the French

Asylum seekers at Sangatte refugee camp, in France. Opened in 1999, the camp is close to the Channel Tunnel which many asylum seekers to enter, hoping to reach England. In January 2002, Eurotunnel launched court actions to have the camp closed down.

A boat carrying 20 illegal immigrants is intercepted off the coast of Fuerteventura, one of the Canary Islands, in April 2000. Spanish authorities are struggling to cope with a large rise in numbers of illegal immigrants.

entrance to the Channel Tunnel has been at the center of controversy because of attempts by some of its refugees to escape through the tunnel to Britain.

What is people trafficking?

Refugees are often desperate, and their desperation can be exploited by people traffickers. These are criminals who smuggle people across borders in return for payment. People trafficking is one of the fastest-growing crimes. It can often start as an opportunist crime, when truck drivers or boat crews receive and accept requests to smuggle people into another country. But in many countries, it has grown rapidly into a network of serious crime involving corrupt border officials. Many refugees transported by people traffickers find themselves caught up in this crime network. For example, some are forced to work as prostitutes on their arrival. Even in Western Europe, where border patrols have been increased and laws tightened, people trafficking is on the increase.

Why Don't Governments Do More?

Refugees and asylum seekers have obligations. For example, they must respect and act within the laws of the country they are staying in. They also have rights. Their most fundamental right is that of "seeking and enjoying" asylum, found in the 1951 UN Convention on the Status of Refugees.

THIS INTERNATIONAL agreement suggests that countries should help refugees, but it does not force them to assist. Many governments choose not to grant asylum to many of those who seek it. Some refuse to resettle refugees within their own country, and sometimes try to force them back to their home country.

Do governments do enough? In all but a small number of less-wealthy African, Asian, and Middle Eastern countries, who already harbor the majority of the world's refugees, the simple answer is "no." Wealthy, industrialized countries give millions of pounds in aid, and offer donations to bodies such as the UNHCR. But some argue that they could afford to

Border police in wealthy European countries report increases in the numbers of people attempting to cross illegally. These Romanians are being held in custody by the German border police.

On the deck of the Norwegian freighter, the MV Tampa, 434 asylum seekers huddle together, with no toilet facilities and just two tarpaulins to protect them from the blazing tropical sun.

give a lot more to help nations struggling with huge numbers of refugees. They could also offer asylum to more refugees.

Many refugees cannot return home, or are unwilling to, because they would face continued persecution. The UNHCR and other organizations attempt to find these people new homes — either in the country they are living in, or in a new host country. But the number who want to resettle is far greater than the number of places available. Many nations agree to accept refugees on a temporary basis during the early phases of a crisis. But only a few — including the U.S., Canada, Sweden and Norway — have regular programs through which they accept a quota (an agreed number) of refugees every year.

Why are governments reluctant to help?

Many of the world's governments are democratically elected e.g. voted in by people at free elections. Politicians try to make decisions that are popular with the voting public so that they have a strong chance of being re-elected. In many powerful countries, there is a large

percentage of the population that dislikes or fears an increase in the number of immigrants. They do not want to see more refugees and asylum seekers allowed into their country. Therefore, politicians sometimes see helping refugees and asylum seekers as a "vote loser."

Winning votes in Australia

In 2001, the Australian prime minister John Howard prevented the MV *Tampa*, a ship carrying over 400 asylum seekers predominantly from Afghanistan, from landing in Australia. A deal to take them elsewhere was agreed. Although there was criticism of his tough policy from inside and outside of the country, Howard's popularity in Australia increased.

Source: Reuters, BBC News

Tragedy struck one attempt at trafficking refugees into Britain, when 54 Chinese men and four Chinese women died of suffocation inside this truck. The bodies were found inside the Dutch container truck after it had crossed the English Channel in June 2000.

Should charity begin at home?

Some people take the view that "charity begins at home." In other words, they think that money and resources should be targeted at their country's own problems. Despite a global news media, where the latest crisis on one side of the world reaches television sets on the other, many people are more concerned with domestic issues that affect them directly. There are, of course, people in need in even the wealthiest nations, — but should charity be restricted by national boundaries?

Some argue that it is the moral duty of wealthy societies to help those in desperate need, wherever they may be. The desperation felt by many refugees and asylum seekers is reflected in the dangerous ways in which some attempt to flee their home country or enter

Refused asylum

Arrested and tortured for several months in Tanzania for being a member of an opposition political party, Adoui Bakkari sought asylum in Britain. In 2001, his application was turned down and he faced deportation. He said: "Death is waiting for me. All I want to say is please let me stay. I am settled here... if I go back to Tanzania I really believe I might be killed."

Source: The Scotsman, *2001*

Between 1892 and 1924, over 22 million people arrived at Ellis Island near the Statue of Liberty to try to enter the U.S. Part of the inscription on the statue reads: "Give me your tired, your poor, your huddled masses yearning to breath free."

another. Between 1996 and 2000, over 600 people drowned, suffocated, or froze to death trying to enter European countries.

Millions are spent in wealthy countries on monuments, parks, and other projects. While these are pleasant additions to a country, some argue that this money could be channeled outside of the country to help save lives.

What reasons are there to help?

Many countries have signed international agreements on refugees. Some people feel that these countries should fully honor the spirit of the agreements by providing homes for refugees. Some countries, such as Britain, France, and Spain, have grown rich by exploiting the resources of less-developed countries when they were colonial powers. Other countries, such as the U.S. and Germany, have relied on massive immigration to fill labor shortages or to rebuild their countries after major conflicts. Shouldn't countries acknowledge help they have received in the past by assisting countries in need today?

What is the arms trade?

The arms trade is another issue. Land mines and other weapons which maim and kill help to create thousands of refugees. These arms also make huge amounts of money for companies and governments of richer countries.

Is this just the nature of business? Or should more of the wealth that is generated from the arms trade, including the profits made and the taxes collected, be used directly to help victims?

Are we being swamped by refugees?

When people flee their own country and seek sanctuary in another, they apply for "asylum." This means the right to be recognized as a refugee. There are approximately one million asylum applications under consideration globally and these are rising steadily. People and governments of countries with large numbers of asylum applications fear that increasing numbers would become a burden they could not bear.

The number of refugees and asylum seekers compared to the overall population is often smaller than imagined. For example, in 2000 the U.K. held 129,000 asylum seekers, and 132,700 people who had been granted refugee status in the past ten years. This was out of a total population of over 58 million. However, even such relatively small numbers, though, have an impact on society. The government must meet the cost of looking after refugees and providing them with social services. There is also fear among many people that new arrivals will take their jobs. This fear is greatest at times of economic difficulty. Yet, most refugees and asylum seekers find work in what is known as the "3d sector"– with the d's standing for the dirty, dangerous, and difficult tasks in low-paid jobs which others refuse.

Can social services cope?

Asylum seekers do tend to need extra support and help, especially when they first arrive. This can cause resentment among the larger population, who think asylum seekers are unlikely to contribute greatly in the future. Many see the typical profile of an asylum seeker as a poor, uneducated, adult male. The majority of asylum seekers are male, but almost half are children and many are educated.

Even after surviving their journey to a new country, many refugees face the heartbreak of being sent home against their will. Here, refugees from Vietnam stage a protest in Hong Kong against enforced repatriation.

A security official in Hong Kong checks the papers of a Vietnamese mother being repatriated to Vietnam.

What is enforced repatriation?

Repatriation means going home. Enforced repatriation means sending people home against their will. The 1951 UN Convention protects refugees against enforced repatriation if they are likely to face persecution. This protection is called "non-refoulement." But for an asylum seeker whose application fails, there is no such protection. After all avenues of appeal have failed, asylum seekers are often sent home. There, they may well face an uncertain and dangerous future.

DEBATE - If we accept more refugees, won't we be flooded with applications?

- Yes. If countries loosen laws allowing people in, and decide in favor of more asylum applications, it will open the floodgates. Thousands of displaced people will flock to countries with friendlier laws.
- No. Governments can still set a maximum limit on how many people they will accept each year. Passing stricter laws on asylum seekers does not necessarily stop massive increases in asylum applications. In the U.K., despite stricter policies, the number of asylum seekers rose by 54 percent between 1998 and 1999.

Aren't most asylum seekers bogus?

Deciding who is, and who is not, a refugee can be complex and difficult. Cases have to be investigated closely to see if someone has "a well-founded fear of persecution." Wealthier nations in Europe and North America grant refugee status to fewer than half of the asylum seekers who apply.

Asylum seekers whose applications are turned down by a government are increasingly labeled as "bogus." This is a highly-charged word which implies that the person is dishonest or was in some way attempting to cheat the system in order to obtain a higher standard of living. It is true that some claims for asylum are groundless. But a large number of the adults who seek asylum, including many whose applications are rejected, have suffered human rights abuses and other forms of persecution. In many host countries, between 15 percent and 35 percent of those who are not granted refugee status are still allowed to remain on "humanitarian grounds."

How are asylum seekers treated?

Until their cases have been heard, most asylum seekers are denied rights which are available to the country's ordinary citizens. These can include the right to work. Asylum seekers in wealthy countries are held either in detention centers or housed in basic conditions awaiting the government's decisions. A decision can take months, even years, leaving asylum seekers facing the constant fear of being sent home while holding a position of very low status in the host country.

In Britain, for example, most financial aid given to asylum seekers has come in the form of vouchers. These are valid for four weeks and can only be used in certain stores. Oxfam and the Refugee Council, among others, think vouchers humiliate asylum seekers and mark them out as targets for prejudice.

One young woman told Oxfam that receiving vouchers was "like getting a stamp saying you don't belong."

Extreme right-wing protesters frequently target refugees and asylum seekers, accusing them of being bogus and representing a drain on resources.

A Turkish man struggles as British police officers forcibly eject him from the country.

Failed asylum seeker dies

On September 21, 1998 Semira Adamu, a 20-year-old Nigerian woman whose asylum application had failed, was forced aboard a flight from Belgium. When she started to struggle and scream, her police escort held a cushion over her face for fifteen minutes. She died from suffocation.

Source: Agence France Presse

Most asylum seekers arrive poor and in need, but some may have been wealthy in the past. Taking flight can mean leaving behind everything you own or having it taken from you, including money and savings. Wars and persecution often cut across class and education boundaries, forcing people from all walks of life — from peasant farmers to lawyers and doctors — to flee. Although asylum seekers require aid on arrival, their skills and knowledge may be of positive benefit in the future.

A pie chart, based on UN figures, showing the percentage of total asylum applications received in the year 2000 by the major richer countries.

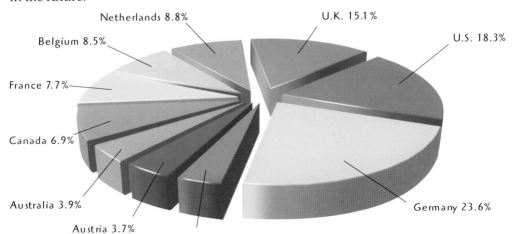

Netherlands 8.8%
Belgium 8.5%
France 7.7%
Canada 6.9%
Australia 3.9%
Austria 3.7%
Switzerland 3.5%
U.K. 15.1%
U.S. 18.3%
Germany 23.6%

What Problems Do Refugees Face In Their New Homes?

Most refugees arrive in a new country with few possessions but plenty of terrible experiences seared into their memories. Making a fresh start in a new country is rarely the end of a refugee's struggles.

REFUGEES CAN ENCOUNTER kindness and help, but they may also encounter prejudice, language difficulties, as well as verbal and physical abuse. They start their new lives in need of shelter and numbers of refugees may be all housed in one area. Alternatively, a host government may decide to disperse them around the country. In whatever way they are distributed, refugees usually find themselves in the most basic housing in the poorest areas.

DEBATE - Should refugees all be housed in the same area?

- Yes. Grouping refugees together gives them an immediate network of support, providing neighbors from their own background. This is especially important in the early stages, and helps refugees to feel safe.
- No. Native populations resent the creation of "ghettos" full of refugees. Dispersing refugees makes it harder for them at first, but it gives them a better chance of integrating into the society of their new country.

A young refugee from Kosovo begins her journey to Germany in 1999. Around 91,000 refugees from Kosovo were moved to other countries at this time.

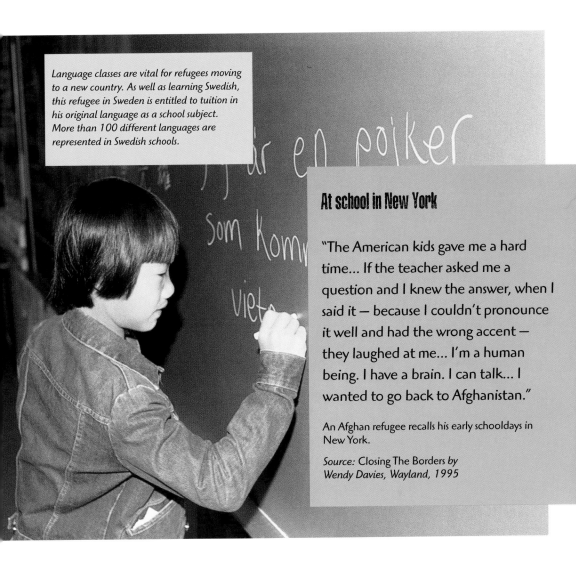

Language classes are vital for refugees moving to a new country. As well as learning Swedish, this refugee in Sweden is entitled to tuition in his original language as a school subject. More than 100 different languages are represented in Swedish schools.

At school in New York

"The American kids gave me a hard time... If the teacher asked me a question and I knew the answer, when I said it — because I couldn't pronounce it well and had the wrong accent — they laughed at me... I'm a human being. I have a brain. I can talk... I wanted to go back to Afghanistan."

An Afghan refugee recalls his early schooldays in New York.

Source: Closing The Borders by Wendy Davies, Wayland, 1995

Why is language a barrier?

Communication is a fundamental human activity. Refugees arriving in a country where they don't know the language face huge problems. If their own language is not understood, they can find it hard to express their needs and obtain vital information.

Many host countries provide support for learning a new language. Refugees in Sweden, for example, are granted 240 hours of free language tuition. But even with assistance, it can be very difficult for adults to learn a completely new language. As a result, finding work becomes harder. Surveys in the U.S. and Southeast Asia show that refugees who speak the local language are twice as likely to find work. They are also far more likely to obtain higher-paid jobs.

Young refugees tend to pick up a new language more quickly than adults, and they are often able to act as interpreters for their parents. However, when children have problems learning a new language, it often slows their education and makes it very difficult for them to fit in at a new school.

Some immigrants have to contend with abuse, vandalism, and threats. This home in Stepney, London, has been daubed with anti–immigrant graffiti in an attempt to stop an Asian family moving into a mainly white area.

Attacks on refugees in Scotland

The Scottish Refugee Council (SRC) reported 70 racially-motivated attacks against asylum seekers and refugees housed in Sighthill, Glasgow between August 2000 and January 2001. In August 2001, a Turkish refugee named Firsat Dag was stabbed to death in an unprovoked attack. An SRC spokeswoman said: "It is scandalous that people's lives are being threatened in Glasgow when they have come here for safety."

Sources: BBC News, The Scotsman and Human Rights Watch

What other barriers are there?

Some refugees move to new continents in order to seek sanctuary. Refugees from cold Tibet who are accepted into Australia, and those from tropical Asia or Africa who settle in Norway or Canada, are among those adjusting to a massive change in climate. The food that a refugee is used to eating may not be available in their new country, or might be too expensive for them to afford. Refugees also miss the culture, arts, music, and news of their home — as they can struggle to pick up the foreign ways of their host country.

Highly-educated refugees with professions or trades may already speak their host country's language. But they often have to retrain or seek new qualifications before they can work in their chosen field — if they get the chance at all. In the meantime, they have to take whatever jobs they can. This often means that refugees end up working in low-paid industries or doing part-time, unofficial work where there is a great threat of exploitation.

How does racism affect refugees?

Refugees may be accepted into a new country officially, but they are not always accepted by the entire population. Refugees are often placed in areas where the poorest people live. Their arrival can upset local people in need, particularly if refugees appear to cut in line for social services.
In times of economic difficulties, this resentment can spill over into discrimination and abuse. Refugees are often used as scapegoats by racists, those who believe that certain races are superior or inferior to others. Many refugees live in fear of racist attacks.

DEBATE – Should social services put the needs of refugees first?

- No. Refugees are often given priority for housing and other benefits. The people they jump ahead of are also very deserving of help, have lived there all their lives, and may have been waiting for much longer.
- Yes. Refugees who are resettled in a country are now citizens of that country and have the same rights as all other citizens. Assistance should be given to those citizens most in need, which is often the refugees.

Turkish refugees take part in a funeral procession for three Turkish women in the northern German town of Mölln. The women were burned to death in their homes during a firebomb attack by German youths.

AUSLÄNDER RAUS!

Can refugees resettle happily?

Many people believe that refugees can never truly settle in their host country. They point as proof to media quotes of refugees wishing to leave, reports of crimes committed by refugees, and the many refugees who require counseling and help long after their arrival. It is true that, after all their experiences, adjusting to a new way of life is hard for many refugees. But what makes the headlines far less is the fact that large numbers of refugees manage to adapt, settle, and flourish in their new environment.

The media often features tales of refugees unhappy with aspects of their host country or the treatment they have received. Often their criticism may be valid, but it can give the impression that most refugees are ungrateful. A more balanced view would be achieved if an equal amount of coverage was given to the many refugees who are happy with, and thankful for, their new home.

Can refugees build a new life?

There are thousands of cases of refugees who settle and integrate successfully into their new country. Some go on to make outstanding contributions to their new country. There are a number of famous examples. Canada's first ever foreign-born Governor-General, Adrienne Clarkson, was a refugee forced to flee from Hong Kong during the Second World War. The successful British internet businessman Sieng Van Tran was one of the Vietnamese boat people of the 1970s. On five separate

A refugee from Vietnam receives instruction on computers at the San Jose Elementary School in Jacksonville, Florida.

Winner of the 1992 Nobel Peace Prize, Rigoberta Menchu's controversial autobiography graphically recounts many examples of the abuse and violence which devastated her local community.

occasions, the Nobel Peace Prize has been won by a refugee. In 1992, it was awarded to Rigoberta Menchu, a Quiche Indian woman who was a refugee from Guatemala. And for every famous refugee, there are hundreds more who have made positive contributions to the local areas in which they have settled.

Some people continue to see refugees purely as victims: people in need who are a drain on resources. Others, however, look at refugees as remarkable people who have survived by virtue of their courage, persistence, and ingenuity — qualities valued in most countries. The challenge for governments is to find ways of integrating refugees successfully and happily into their societies.

Thankful

Shukri Sindi, a Kurdish boy, was 14 when he and his family were forced to flee from the oppression of the Iraqi government. A gifted artist, Sindi spent three years in a refugee camp where he never had the use of a pen or paper. After being allowed into the U.S., Sindi has flourished. He is now a student studying for a degree in architecture. In Arabic his name means "thankful," and more than anything else he is thankful for the opportunities he and his family have been given.

Source: American Kurdish Information Network (AKIN)

Do Refugees Ever Return Home?

The most fervent wish expressed by refugees all over the world is for an end to the troubles and problems that forced them to seek refuge away from their homelands. The drive to return is strong in almost all refugees.

MILLIONS OF REFUGEES remain exiled from their country of origin. Some integrate into the country in which they first sought asylum, others resettle in different host countries and build a new life there. A large number of the world's refugees today are held in detention centers and refugee camps outside their own country's borders.

But some refugees do travel back home and try to pick up the pieces of their former lives. They often experience both happiness and hardship on their return. In 2000, around 800,000 refugees were repatriated — returning to their home country. The desire to go home can be so strong that many refugees return to their country of origin even when major fears

Returning home is a cause of celebration for these pre-school children in Sri Lanka. Organizations such as the UNHCR attempt to smooth the path for refugees to return and pick up the threads of their former lives.

A Bosnian family are reunited in Sarajevo in 1997, after having spent more than four years apart.

for their safety remain. For example, despite ongoing violence and troubles, over 30,000 refugees chose to return to Sierra Leone in 2000.

Returning home can be as difficult for refugees as settling in a new country. Their experiences have altered their lives in a major and dramatic way, and they have to try to deal with the trauma they have been through. The happiness of being reunited with friends and family may be mixed with grief for relatives who have been killed since the refugees fled.

Returning refugees have to rebuild their lives, not only emotionally but also physically and socially. They have to settle back in to their former culture, and to a place which may have changed greatly. They have to rebuild houses and facilities, and to seek out work. Some help may be given to returning refugees by international aid agencies and by local governments and communities, but the real effort has to be made by the returning refugees themselves.

Return to Kosovo

"We returned because it is our land," said Sreten Djuric, one of 80 Serbian refugees who returned to Kosovo in September 2001 in a scheme organized by the UNHCR. The main village in the valley is just a building site, with lumber and bricks on the roadside. Many of the Serbs have learned how to lay bricks and build roofs, and are working hard to make their homes habitable before the harsh winter arrives. In the meantime, they live in tents and receive food from aid groups. They have no electricity or running water. Astrid van Genderen Stort, a UNHCR spokeswoman, stated: "The way this project has been handled, and how it is going so far, does raise hope."

Source: Reuters

REFERENCE

ESTIMATED NUMBER OF REFUGEES
(BY CONTINENT)

Africa

1951	5,000
1961	6,500
1971	991,900
1981	3,026,000
1991	5,277,700
1999	3,523,100

Asia

1951	41,500
1961	6,500
1971	203,400
1981	4,677,900
1991	8,518,700
1999	4,781,800

Europe

1951	1,221,200
1961	775,800
1971	617,500
1981	587,900
1991	1,564,400
1999	2,617,700

Latin America and the Caribbean

1951	120,000
1961	120,000
1971	209,900
1981	405,800
1991	899,400
1999	61,100

North America

1951	518,500
1961	544,500
1971	547,200
1981	1,099,400
1991	683,700
1999	649,600

Oceania

1951	180,000
1961	nil
1971	38,000
1981	327,800
1991	76,000
1999	64,500

World

1951	2,116,200
1961	1,476,300
1971	2,750,900
1981	10,194,900
1991	17,022,000
1999	11,697,800

Source: UNHCR

NUMBER OF PERSONS OF CONCERN
TO UNHCR (1990–2001)

According to the UNHCR, there are approximately 50 million people uprooted from their homes all over the world. Just under half this number are of concern to the UNHCR.

1990	14,916,498
1991	17,209,722
1992	17,007,483
1993	18,998,777
1994	23,033,000
1995	27,437,000
1996	26,103,200
1997	22,729,000
1998	22,376,300
1999	21,459,620
2000	22,257,340
2001	21,793,300

Source: UNHCR

NUMBER OF PERSONS OF CONCERN TO UNHCR (BY REGION)

January 1, 2000

Asia	7,308,860
Africa	6,250,540
Europe	7,285,800
North America	1,241,930
Latin America and Caribbean	90,170
Oceania	80,040
Total	22,257,340

January 1, 2001

Asia	8,450,000
Africa	6,072,900
Europe	5,571,700
North America	1,047,100
Latin America and Caribbean	575,600
Oceania	76,000
Total	21,793,300

Source: UNHCR

REFUGEE RESETTLEMENT BY HOST COUNTRY (2000)

United States	72,500
Canada	13,500
Australia	6,600
Sweden	1,500
Norway	1,500
Finland	760
New Zealand	700
Denmark	460
Japan	140

Source: UNHCR

TEN LARGEST REFUGEE POPULATIONS (1999)

Country of Origin	Number	Main Countries of Asylum
Afghanistan	3,580,400	Pakistan and Iran
Burundi	568,000	Tanzania
Iraq	512,000	Iran
Sudan	490,400	Uganda, Democratic Republic of Congo, Ethiopia, Kenya, Chad, and Central African Republic
Bosnia-Herzegovina	478,300	Yugoslavia and Croatia
Somalia	447,800	Kenya, Ethiopia, Yemen, and Djibouti
Angola	432,700	Zambia, Namibia and Democratic Republic of Congo
Sierra Leone	400,800	Guinea and Liberia
Eritrea	376,400	Sudan
Vietnam	370,300	China

(Note: Nearly four million Palestinians are not included in these figures.)
Source: UNHCR

APPROXIMATE ESTIMATES OF INTERNALLY DISPLACED PERSONS (DECEMBER 2000)

The numbers of people internally displaced inside a country are extremely hard to count, as many people may be in hiding and not reachable by international monitors.

Sudan	4,000,000
Angola	1,100,000–3,800,000
Colombia	2,100,000
Congo-Kinshasa	1,800,000
Myanmar (Burma)	600,000–1,000,000
Sierra Leone	500,000–1,000,000
Turkey	400,000–1,000,000
Indonesia	750,000–850,000
Iraq	700,000
Burundi	600,000
Sri Lanka	600,000
Azerbaijan	575,000
Bosnia-Herzegovina	518,000
India	507,000
Syria	500,000
Uganda	500,000
Russian Federation	490,000
Yugoslavia	480,000
Afghanistan	375,000
Lebanon	300,000–350,000
Eritrea	310,000
Somalia	300,000
Ethiopia	280,000
Georgia	272,000
Cyprus	265,000
Israel	200,000–250,000
Algeria	100,000–200,000
Philippines	150,000
Rwanda	150,000
Kenya	100,000
North Korea	100,000
Bangladesh	60,000
Peru	60,000
Croatia	34,000
Congo-Brazzaville	30,000
Solomon Islands	30,000
Liberia	20,000
Gaza Strip and West Bank	17,000
Mexico	16,000

Source: World Refugee Survey

REFUGEE POPULATIONS BY MAIN COUNTRY OF ASYLUM (1999)

Islamic Republic of Iran	1,835,700
Pakistan	202,000
Germany	975,500
Tanzania	622,200
United States	513,000
Guinea	501,500
Yugoslavia	500,700
Sudan	391,000
Armenia	296,200
China	293,300
Democratic Republic of Congo	285,200
Ethiopia	257,700
Kenya	223,700
Azerbaijan	221,600
Uganda	218,200
Zambia	206,400
India	180,000
Algeria	165,200
Indonesia	162,500
Sweden	159,500
France	140,200
Ivory Coast	138,400
Canada	136,600
United Kingdom	132,700
Netherlands	129,100
Iraq	128,900
Nepal	127,900
Switzerland	111,600
Thailand	100,100
Liberia	96,300

Source: UNHCR

RATIO OF REFUGEES TO HOST COUNTRY POPULATION (END OF 2000)

Host Country

Yugoslavia	1 refugee per 22 people
Iran	1 refugee per 36 people
Pakistan	1 refugee per 75 people
Sudan	1 refugee per 76 people
Uganda	1 refugee per 101 people
Thailand	1 refugee per 285 people
Germany	1 refugee per 456 people
Canada	1 refugee per 566 people
U.S.	1 refugee per 572 people
U.K.	1 refugee per 681 people
Indonesia	1 refugee per 1,754 people
Japan	1 refugee per 33,395 people

Source: World Refugee Survey 2001

Major Voluntary Repatriations (2000)

During 2000, an estimated 800,000 refugees returned from their countries of asylum to their home countries. This was well-down on the previous year's figure. In 1999, 1.6 million refugees, including 800,000 people from Kosovo, were repatriated.

From	Returning To	Number
Pakistan and Iran	Afghanistan	209 600
Bosnia, Germany, Turkey, and others	Yugoslavia	88 500
Ethiopia, Djibouti, and others	Somalia	75 000
Sudan	Eritrea	50 000
Indonesia	East Timor	40 000
Ivory Coast and Guinea	Liberia	40 000
Guinea and Liberia	Sierra Leone	35 000
Congo-Kinshasa and Tanzania	Rwanda	25 000
Germany, Croatia, Yugoslavia, and others	Bosnia-Herzegovina	19 000
Yugoslavia	Croatia	17 000
Congo-Kinshasa	Congo-Brazzaville	10 000
Tanzania	Burundi	10 000
Rwanda and Central African Republic	Congo-Kinshasa	7000
Congo-Kinshasa	Angola	6000
Ethiopia	Kenya	5000
Kazakhstan and others	Tajikistan	4500
Gambia, Senegal, and others	Guinea-Bissau	3000–5000
Iran	Iraq	3600
Djibouti and Sudan	Ethiopia	3000
Cameroon and others	Chad	2500
Bangladesh	Myanmar (Burma)	1300
Senegal	Mauritania	1000

Source: World Refugee Survey

Major New People Displacements (1999–2000)

Afghanistan	250,000 new Afghan IDPs, and 172,000 flee to Pakistan.
Angola	300,000 Angolans uprooted by ongoing civil war.
Burundi	150,000 Burundians flee from atrocities and civil war.
Colombia	315,000 Colombians newly displaced by political violence, of which 266,000 leave the country.
Congo-Kinshasa	Approximately one million people flee war and atrocities.
Eritrea	750,000 Eritreans displaced by border war with Ethiopia.
Guinea	60,000 Guineans flee due to cross-border attacks by rebels.
Indonesia	800,000 Indonesians displaced by religious and ethnic violence.
Kosovo	9,900 people newly displaced.
Liberia	50,000 flee attacks by rebels and retaliation by soldiers.
Philippines	800,000 people displaced, 650,000 of whom return home.
Sierra Leone	210,000 Sierra Leoneans flee renewed atrocities and civil war.
Sri Lanka	230,000 displaced, and 1,600 more flee to India.
Sudan	100,000 Sudanese displaced by aerial bombings and civil war.
Uganda	120,000 newly uprooted by insurgency and atrocities.

Source: World Refugee Survey/U.S. Committee For Refugees

GLOSSARY

Aborigines Original inhabitants of a country, particularly Australia.

asylum A place of safety and refuge provided by a host country to refugees.

asylum seekers People who have applied for refugee status and are waiting to see if they will be granted protection as a refugee.

chemotherapy A treatment for cancer.

citizen A member of a country or other political community.

civilians People who are not in the armed forces.

civil rights Basic rights of everyone, including freedom and equality.

civil war A war between opposing groups within one country.

conscience Moral sense of right and wrong. Freedom of conscience means free choice of religion.

convention A legal agreement to behave in a certain way, made between two or more countries.

democracy Government by all the people. In practice, rule by a government voted into power in free elections.

deportation The forced removal of a person from one country to another.

detention center A place where asylum seekers are held while their cases are investigated.

domestic Of the home, or of your home country.

emigrant A person who leaves their own country to settle in another country.

ethnic group A group of people of the same race or culture, often a minority in a country.

forced labor Forcing people to work, usually in terrible conditions.

forced relocation Forcing people to move away from their homes.

genocide The deliberate attempt to kill all of the members of a racial, ethnic, or religious group.

ghetto An area of a town or city where a minority group are forced to live.

host country A country which receives refugees.

human rights The basic rights of all human beings, such as the right to free speech, food, and shelter.

hypothermia A medical condition where the body temperature drops, causing bodily functions to shut down.

IDP (internally displaced person) A person who has been forced from their home, but is still within their home country's borders.

immigrant Someone who arrives from abroad to settle in a new country.

infamous Famous for being vile or evil, notorious.

integration The combining of different parts, particularly the mixing of different groups in a society on the basis of equality.

land mine A bomb which explodes when it is stepped on.

malaria Type of fever transmitted by the bite of an Anopheles mosquito.

malnutrition Lack of foods necessary for good health.

migrant Someone who moves from one region or country to another.

Muslim Someone who follows the Islamic religion.

non-refoulement The right of refugees under international law not to be forced to return to the country they fled from.

persecution The harassment and mistreatment of a particular person or group of people because of their beliefs.

pneumonia Inflammation of the lungs.

popular uprising A revolt or revolution led by the ordinary people of a country.

racism Beliefs and actions based on the idea that one racial group is superior to another.

refuge A place of shelter from pursuit or danger.

refugee Person taking refuge, especially in a foreign country, to escape such troubles as religious or political persecution and war.

repatriation Return of people to their country of origin.

retaliation Returning punishment in kind, or fighting back.

right-wing Having conservative beliefs, which in extreme cases can involve extreme nationalism and racism.

sanctuary A place of safety, free from harm or the threat of harm.

sanitation Systems which provide fresh water and remove garbage and sewage.

scapegoat A person or group unfairly blamed for the problems or actions of others.

social services The provision of housing, health, and education services by the state.

transit camp A temporary home for refugees while they wait either to be resettled elsewhere or to return to their original country.

trauma An extremely powerful or terrible shock.

UN (United Nations) An international organization, founded in 1945, in which representatives from most of the world's nations meet to discuss conflicts and try to work towards peace.

UNHCR The office of the United Nations High Commissioner for Refugees, set up by the UN to deal with the problem of refugees.

visa A document or stamp in a passport allowing a person to visit or stay in a country.

FURTHER INFORMATION

0

BOOKS and MAGAZINES

Past and Present: Refugees by Carole Seymour-Jones (Heinemann, 1992) This book examines many major refugee crises from the distant past through to modern times.

Refugee Teenagers (UNHCR Public Information Section, 1999) A 24-page color booklet for teenagers about refugee teenagers, dealing with exile and featuring personal accounts. Available from UNHCR, Public Information Section, CP 2500, 1211 Geneva 2 Depot, Switzerland.

Refugees by Rachel Warner (Wayland, 1996) Written by an Education Officer at the Minority Rights Group, this is an interesting account of the refugee situation told through case studies from different parts of the world.

Refugees and Asylum Seekers edited by Craig Donnellan (Independence Educational Publishers, 1999) A resources book with reports, articles, and surveys from a range of newspapers, government departments, and charitable organizations.

The State of the World's Refugees 2000 edited by Mark Cutts (Office of the United Nations High Commissioner for Refugees, Oxford University Press, 2000) An in-depth look at the major refugee crises of the past 50 years and how responses to refugees have changed over that time. The book carries many up-to-date tables of statistics.

ORGANIZATIONS

American Refugee Committee
430 Oak Grove St, Suite 204,
Minneapolis, MN 55403
email: archq@archq.org
website: www.archq.org

CARE
CARE International is one of the world's largest private humanitarian organizations, with 11 national organizations and regional offices across the U.S.
CARE International, 151 Ellis Street, NE Atlanta, Georgia 30303–2440
email: info@care.org
website:www.careusa.org

European Council on Refugees and Exiles (ECRE)
An organization of 72 refugee-assisting agencies in 28 countries, concerned with the humane treatment of asylum seekers and refugees.
ECRE Secretariat, Clifton Centre, Unit 22, 3rd Floor, 110 Clifton Street, London EC2A 4HT, UK
Email: ecre@ecre.org

International Committee of the Red Cross (ICRC)
The ICRC helps to direct relief work and assistance provided to refugees by other agencies.
Public Information Centre, 19 Avenue de la Paix, CH 1202, Genève, Switzerland
website: www.icrc.org

Oxfam America
26 West street, Boston, MA 0211
website: www.oxfamamerica.org

Refugees International
An organization working to save lives of
refugees in all parts of the world via aid
programmes and projects.
Refugees International, 1705 N Street,
NW, Washington DC, 20036
email: ri@refintl.org
website: www.refintl.org

**United Nations High Commissioner
for Refugees (UNHCR)**
The international organization set up in
1951 to provide physical assistance to
refugees as well as providing protection
in law.
UNHCR, 1775 K St, NW #300,
Washington DC, 20006
website: www.unhcr.ch/cgi-
bin/texis/vtx/home

WEBSITES
www.amnesty.org
Amnesty International, the famous
human rights charitable organization.
This website features reports,
documents, and details of the latest
Amnesty campaigns.

www.exileimages.co.uk
An unusual photo library devoted to
pictures of refugees and development
aid complete with photo case stories of
refugees from all over the world.

www.hrw.org/refugees
Human Rights Watch, an organization
dedicated to monitoring the human
rights conditions in many countries.

www.idpproject.org
Set up by the Norwegian Refugee
Council, the Global IDP Project looks
at the issue of internally displaced
persons and provides assistance and
information.

www.refugeecamp.org
A graphic and informative look at
refugee camps, how they operate, and
the difficulties camp organizers and
refugees face.

www.refugeecouncil.org.uk
The web pages of the largest refugee and
asylum seeker organization in Britain.

www.refugees.org
The home page of the U.S. Committee
for Refugees has maps and background
information on many regions generating
refugees. Refugees' stories can be heard
as sound files.

INDEX